Mommy,
WHAT WERE YOU REALLY SAYING?

BY
GERTRUDE GREEN BRODERICK

ISBN: 979-8-9884486-2-4

Publishing By: DemiCo National, LLC

www.DemiCoNational.com

4

TABLE OF CONTENTS

ACKNOWLEDGEMENTS

When the very thought of writing this book came to my mind, I thought again and said, "But I don't even like to write, Lord, and I have never written a book before." So, I tried to suppress the idea of writing this book. That went on for years until around 2017. The idea tugged at my heart again, but like before, I tried to ignore it. The thought kept running through my mind, but I would not give into it. Finally, God allowed a man to enter my life. IIis namc is Captain Andrc Farley. I met him in 2016.

We became close friends. He noticed me quoting my mom. I would always say something like, "Well, mommy would say". Andre would ask me what was that you just said, and I would repeat it with emphasis. Andre said, "Trudy, you are always quoting your mommy sayings, and that is why you need to put it in a book. Trudy, you need to write a book about all the things you've heard your mommy say." I would just laugh it off. But one day I was at home and the thought of placing some of my mom's adages in a book started to become so strong in my spirit. The very next day when I saw Andre, he mentioned writing the book to me and I told him, Andre, I was just thinking the same thing. I said, Andre, I don't know anything about writing a book. He assured me that he did know a thing or two about writing a book and he would be there for me every step of the way. Most of what my mom said was funny to Andre, and he said much of what my mom said made sense. Most of all, Andre would say to me, "Trudy, you need to write a book."

Thank you, Captain Andre Farley, for stirring up the gift that was dormant within me. You motivated me to take a chance and reach beyond the break in the rope. Every time I wanted to put myself down, you would put me in check until I realized what I was doing. I will always be grateful to you for being my human mirror. When I thought I couldn't, you said, "I could do anything I set my mind to do." Truly, you are my hero.

I called her Nurse White. Thank you so much Mrs. Flo White and your sister Linda G. Forrest for supporting me while I was working on my bachelor's degree. I called you both my angel sisters. When I thought I had to drop out of college, both of you came to my rescue and kept me from going under. I will always remember that. Thank you both for sewing into my dream. Nurse White, you have seen me struggle through so much and you were always there to keep me mindful of who I am and to who's I am. That meant the word to me.

Thank you, Professor Altman, for calling out the author in me when I didn't even know I had it in me. Thanks for encouraging me to write after reading my composition in your Springfield College class. Of course, I laughed and said, "No, not me". That was the first time someone ever said that I had a gift to write. Well, I'm still not sure about that, but here I am. You told me I should write a children's book. I'll keep that in the back of my mind. This is not a little children's book, but I do believe children will be able to read it and glean from it.

Thank you, Lisa M. Swinton. I'm not going to hold it against you for having my favorite name, (Michelle). Time will not allow me to thank you in words. Time and space would not be able to contain my gratitude. You supported me all through school and you were my rock when the work got unbearable. You were there to bail me out. You made my homework seem like a game. Thank you so much Lisa.

Thank you, Martha L.S. Green who has long gone on, but thought it not robbery to leave a special part of herself within me. You, through the Holy Spirit, allowed me to internalize Proverbs that have formed me into the person I am now. Martha Lee Simmons Green, Mommy you were the smartest woman I ever knew.

I thank my Lord and Jesus Savior Christ for allowing such wonderful people at the right time to enter my life.

INTRODUCTION

Growing up as the youngest of ten children had its advantages. Since I was the last one left in the house, I was able to spend a lot of time with my mommy. I had the privilege to hear lots of stories and adventures from my mom's life. She would talk about when she was a little girl, and how she had to stand up against some girls in her elementary school that were bullying her sister, brother and even herself. She was not a fighter, but this was one situation that she just could not get around. My mom recounted that as she heard the school bell ring, she also heard a voice echoing in the wind. The voice came from one of the bullies.

She heard a voice yelling, "We are going to kick some a** today!" My mommy told me that she told her sister to brace herself. My mom and her sister had long braids that hung past their shoulders. The girl bullies would run fast behind them, pull them down by their braids, and run over them every day. Mommy always said, if you are going to use a stick as a weapon, never get a stick that is longer than your forearm. She noticed a stick that was just the right length and she reached down and grabbed that stick. As soon as the biggest girl got close, Mommy said she turned around and faced that girl un-expectantly and popped her in the face. The girl went down to the ground, and it was on. To make a long story short, my mom turned the school ground out that day. I'll put it this way.

From that day forth, the Simmons girls were never bullied again thanks to my mom taking a stand. My mom had to stop attending school because as the oldest, she had to go to work so she could help her parents with the little ones. She was the eldest of five siblings. She talked about when she was first married to my dad and how he used to like to step out with the boys and hang out for long hours drinking. One night my dad had a little too much to drink, and he came home "feeling good" as Mommy put it. Apparently, he thought he would let the devil use him to try and hit her. She said that she saw seven devils when that man called himself trying to hit her. She said that she reached into the fireplace and grabbed a fire poker (that's what mom called it). By the time she turned around, my daddy had run out of the house so quickly that she didn't see him pass her. Later that night, my daddy was so afraid to walk through the door first, he had one of his cousins walked through the door ahead of him., My mom said if he would not have called her name first so she could distinguish between the two voices, she would have hit my daddy's cousin in the head. Yes, that was only one of the many, many stories that my mom shared with me.

Every time she shared a story with me, I would always ask her the same question. "Mommy, was I born yet?" She would look at me and say, "No, you were not born yet, baby." I always wanted to make sure mommy would not do anything to stop me from getting here. At least that's the way I saw it in my little mind.

My mom had a saying for almost everything. I know Webster has his words and definitions, and Shakespeare has his poems and rhymes, but my mommy took definitions and meanings to a whole different level. Her words were never recited or revitalized, and that's what I hope to do in this book. My mom's name was Martha Lee. Simmons Green.

Martha was not educated, but she was the most wise and smartest woman I have ever met in this life. Call it motherly consciousness or just being in alignment with her children, but it seemed that my mom knew what we were going to do before we could think about it. She stayed five paces ahead of us. But that was the mothers of yesterday. From my perspective, my mom could have easily written her own dictionary. It might not have passed the board of education, but it surely would have made a good start for a conversation.

My mom told me that a lot of the stuff she said were things that she heard her mom and the older people said when she was a little girl. She went on to say that those things had a way of just staying with her. She was so right because the things that I heard her said stayed with me from a little girl well into my adult life. Those things and the way my mom said them are the main reasons I'm writing this book. The funny thing about it is, I didn't realize how much I had soaked it all in or remembered until a friend of mine reminded me how often I quoted my mom. And another thing, I didn't realize how funny and strong those sayings were.

I'm sure many of you that are from the south might have heard some of these sayings that I'm about to get into as I take a trip down memory lane. My mom was no different from some of your moms. She was a black woman raised in South Carolina from a little place in Goose Creek called Mt. Holey. She spoke what some would consider as broken English and Gullah which gives the pot a much more twisted, but sweet taste.

Not to get too carried away with it, but the Gullah language is truly a big part in the life of the blacks in the south and the islands. Rather than saying, "girl" my people would say, "gal" in the Gullah tongue. You might hear us say, "Come yah" as opposed to saying, "come here." These were the very types of twisted words and phrases that criticized our heritage and helped us establish who we were and who we have become as a people. I hope you will be able to identify, and I pray this book will bring joy to your reading as the many things that I heard mommy say.

CHAPTER ONE

Mommy Talk

My mom was a hard worker. Mommy was a maid in the white people's homes. She was a great maid. The white people would actually wait until my mom got to their home to inform my mom about how their children were misbehaving and acting up. They would expect and respect my mom for getting on their children and disciplining them, and they did not care how mommy handled it. In those days, that was how it went. I was very small and sickly.

Therefore, Mommy would take me with her to work if I was not well enough to attend school. I remembered my mom not getting into her employee's home good before I would hear them calling my mom's name. "Mrs. Martha! Mrs. Martha! Kenny did such and such." By the time my mom got through just talking to the child, tears would start to fall. I thought to myself, little white boy, if you would have only asked me, I would have told you that her bark would make you cry in such a way, you would rather she bite you instead of barking at you. Boy, my mommy had a way of making you cry just by talking. Even though she was uneducated, she believed in working for what she wanted and needed. I always heard my mom and her friends talking about young people working and having something for a rainy day. She would often tell us as children not to run through everything in one day, so we can have something for another day. She would stress the point in having your own.

As a matter of fact, when my sisters became of age for dating, they would bring the guys around. Some of the questions would go like this; "Who is your family? Where are they from? Do you have a job?" My mom was making sure whoever we decided to connect ourselves to was capable of taking care of us and not afraid to work or get their hands dirty. I remember hearing this famous word.

Trifling

Let me break this word down for you. I'm sure if you were raised in the south or on one of the islands, this was a household term. If this word appeared in the same sentence with a guy you were dating, engaged to or even married to, it was not considered a compliment. What my mom and so many mothers in that time were saying was this young man was lazy and did not care about working.

My mom would go as far as to imply he was not a good candidate to take care of a home. As far as my mom's point of view, that word walked close to the term worthless.

I recall my mommy always saying, "I don't pick love for my children." However, if you ever brought a boy home and she found out he couldn't keep a job or he did not like working, you will hear that word used in this context. "Baby, he might be a nice-looking guy from a good family, but he is trifling." "A trifling man will not take care of you." Mommy, what did you mean when you said:

"That boy doesn't have a pot to piss in nor a window to throw it out."

Trust me, this was not a compliment either. I would often hear my mommy and other older people make mention of this cliché. If by any chance, any of the girls brought a boy home that was trifling, most of the time, he would fall in this category also. This adage meant that the person is lacking in a great many things. Not only would this person not be able to be by your side, but they would not even have a side for you to be by. Most of these guys were still living at home with their parents. They were not able to help if their son or daughter got in a pinch.

"That person talks out of both sides of their mouth."

Here we go again. When a person talks out of both sides of their mouth, it is to say that those people are liars. When my mom said that this was the way a person conducted themselves, she was actually saying that they could not be trusted. Mommy said, "Baby, he says one thing one minute, and says something else the next. Don't trust them baby." Sometimes she would say they are talking double. I would be reminded not to let people double talk me. In other words, if they double talk you, they would most likely talk out both sides of their mouth. This too was another household phrase. At least in my house growing up.

Don't you let my mom catch you talking out both sides of your mouth when she asked you whether you had done a certain thing or not. She would actually allow you to plead your case for a while. Yes, notice I said, "for a while." Mommy would not allow you to talk too much especially when she knew you are lying. Sometimes, she would stop you in midair with your story with a swift backhand or a stern vocal lash. Either way, you would realize you were fighting a losing battle.

As a child, it was amazing to me how my mom knew a lie when she heard it. I recall a scripture in the Bible that says, "When I was a child, I spoke as a child, I understood as a child..." (1 Cor. 13:11). That scripture truly explains many things to me now that I am an adult. Like so many children today and the children of yesterday, we did not take into consideration that our parents had traveled the roads we were trying to master. Sometimes, she would say, you sound too believable. Now, this is where a so-called out of body in the mind experience comes into play. Many times, I said to myself after I got far out of her reach, in my mind,

"Man, I'm damned if I do and I'm damned if I don't."

I don't know if you noticed I said all of that in three parts. One, it was said to myself, two, and it was far from her, and three, it was in my own mind. I know you probably think I went to some school to learn that it was wise to approach such a situation in that manner. But no, it was just a matter of learning things the hard way. Somebody out there knows what I'm talking about. One thing you never wanted a black mother to do was to walk up on you while you were talking about them or saying something as if you were the parent. It was as if you had sat down and signed a death wish.

In today's society, a young person might express loudly that their parents are judging or being nosey. Well, don't get me wrong, the children of yesterday thought of saying those things and we did say them. However, we had enough sense to utter those thoughts and ideas far away so that our parents could not hear us. I have found in my time on this earth that it's okay to be nosey as a parent in this world.

When I was growing up, I recall my older siblings telling me about the nosey old people that lived in the neighborhood. These were the type of people that your parents knew had their back. Of course, this was also the type of neighbor that did not want to see you do anything wrong because your parents would find out. And please, don't let them have something that they could use or hold over your head. That was like blackmail.

Sometimes these nosey old people lied, but we were not allowed to say they were liars. That's when the crazy question would surface. It would sound like this, "Oh, Mrs. Reed Lied?" Please don't get it twisted that this was not a time for you to use your freedom of expression. The best thing you could do is just be quiet and look stupid. I know, you're probably thinking that the best response would be to say, "no mam, she isn't a liar." Wrong. You might say, just tell the truth. "Yes, she is a liar." Wrong. You really don't want to respond with the latter because you would get beat down til your next birthday. Now, the first response sounds logical.

Please don't try that either because it was a trick question. If you go with the first one, my mom would say, "That's right, Mrs. Reed don't lie. So, why are you trying to make me think she lie!" In other words, damned if you do and damned if you don't.

"Donkey Fyfe"

If my mom said that a guy was a Donkey Fyfe, she was not calling him gay or anything. She was just saying that he was too soft to do any hard work or to hold up his part of the deal as the man. I often wondered about this saying. As I got older, I understood it completely. Donkey Fyfe from my mom's perspective indicated that this man wanted to stay at home and let the women take care of him. He was one of those men that did not have any shame in his game. As a matter of fact, he didn't mind if his women held down two jobs while he played around.

"Boy won't work in a pie factory."

I'm not sure if working in pie factories was considered easy work back in my mother's day. All I know is whenever my mom said this, again, it was not considered a compliment to the boy. I never thought of asking my mom if she ever worked in a pie factory because she spoke on this subject as if she was an expert. This was the young man or girl that just didn't want to work anywhere. If you brought a job to them that they did not have to go looking for, they would have still turned you down.

Well, at least that was my mom's testimony on the subject. Along with not wanting to work in the pie factory, my mom also said, "If you put a job in his lap, he won't do it." That's when you know a person really doesn't want to work at all.

"He just blows smoke."

This is when a person is just saying something to be saying something. Whenever a young man or young woman goes on and on concerning a subject or a matter, my mom would say that they are not being truthful. Sometimes, she would say that, "Oh, he always says that he is going to do such and such, but he never gets around to doing it."

Mommy would remind whoever is listening not to hold him to his words because all that is, is just words. Sometimes, mommy would pretend to really be listening to the person, but reality check would step in to let that person know that my mom was no dummy. There were so many things I admired about my mommy, but the most thing that I admired was her uncanny way of seeing right through a person.

CHAPTER TWO
Words to boys Words to girls

"That gal (girl) is fast!"

By no means was my mom talking about how fast you could run. Whenever my mom uses this phrase, she meant that as a little girl; she was growing up much too fast, and she was most likely getting into things that were considered for grown folks to be doing. I remember my mom sitting me down and telling me that she did not want me running around with fast girls. Now, I knew what she meant when she used that word because I was raised in her house. I would look into her eyes and say, "Yes Mama." On the other hand, I did not have the heart or the guts to tell her that I was one of the fast gals.

"Don't be chasing frock tails."

My mom had more girls than boys, so most of the time she made statements towards the girls. However, she had two boys among the girls. Therefore, Mom had to focus on things that the boys were doing also. She would make it a point to emphasize that the boys needed to be mindful not to chase after frock tails. Even though it was a natural thing for boys to go after or would want to consider the girls, Mommy just didn't want them considering the girls too soon.

In other words, Mommy knew that the boys would realize that there was a difference between the two genders, but Mommy wanted her boys to respect the girls. She did not want her boys to be bringing any little ones into the world at such a young age. Sometimes, girls were made out to be hot wires while the little boys got off free without thinking that those two genders together can actually start a fire, and as you know, it does take two to tangle.

"Tail between your legs."

As a result, if a boy or a girl was mischievous, and being fast as my mom would say or chasing frock tails, eventually, they would find themselves in a shameful state. That is when one or the other would end up with their tails between their legs. I always wondered about how this saying came about. The analogy was pulled from the actions of a dog when it was scolded for doing something wrong. We had many dogs when I was growing up.

I recall times when my daddy would chastise our dogs for one reason or the other. The dogs would either run away or walk away with their tails between their legs. This was a sign that the dogs were ashamed of what they had done. I remember the dogs running away with that same posture, even if they had gotten beat up by another dog.

It's so amazing to me that something so common as watching dogs react to certain situations can make for an illustration among humans. I heard the comedian Seinfeld say that if an alien looked down on us and saw humans walking behind a dog; while stopping every so often picking up poop from our dogs, one would have to question who is in charge?

Being fast, chasing frock tails, and tail between your legs brings to the front another adage that my mom used to say. Mommy would say,

n

"*That child is boy/girl crazy.*"

Now, you have to know my mommy to really get a full understanding when she made a comment like that. My mom was a low talker and had a sweet spirit. She would rather tie a rope around her neck than to say something bad or mean about someone. When Mommy said this adage, she was not saying that the children had some kind of mental problem. No, she was just stating that all they thought about was the opposite sex all the time while everything else was second nature. She thought that was crazy.

From my mom's perspective, this is what qualifies you as being boy or girl crazy. If you were on the front or back porch talking to a boy and she had to call your name more than twice to get your attention, you were qualified as being boy crazy. If you call yourself having a party and most of the guests on the list were more girls than boys, you qualified as being girl crazy. She wanted it to balance out. If every two words that came out of your mouth had something to do with a boy or girl, you were considered as one that most likely had the boy/girl crazy syndrome. Now, if all of this lined up just right, my mom would remind you of something.

"A hard head makes a soft behind."

I used to really wonder about this one a lot, and the reason for that was my mom acted like she was doing me a favor. So as a child, I used to think that as long as your head was hard, your butt would be soft. Well, in hindsight, she was doing us a favor. As a child, it didn't make too much sense. It took me a while, but before I left her house, I understood. Mommy was saying, "If you continue to be boy or girl crazy, and I have to call you more than one time to get your attention, I'm going to tan your behind.

When I get through with your butt, you will come running to me before the thought of me calling you comes to my mind." Sometimes she would say, 'Ya'll keep making your head hard.``

Please don't get the woman wrong. She was not giving you permission to continue doing the wrong thing. "Making your head hard" was when a child just could not stop being rambunctious. No problem. My mom had a cure for that. My mom did not believe in sparing the rod. That was the time when Mommy would have sent you for a long walk.

The walk included you looking for your own switch. Of course, that was a long walk. If you took too long bringing that switch back, you are going to get double for your trouble. As a child, I could never understand a person making you walk for your own weapon of warfare. At least, looking back on it, that was the way I viewed it.

Let me try to explain it since I'm an adult. Imagine a little child is about to experience a whipping, so the parent sends the child out to look or retrieve their own switch (weapon). The switch that the child brings back to the parent will be the very switch that will be used on their own behind (warfare). It's going to be a war up in that house that will not feel fair. Now do you see my point? Weapon of warfare.

I heard a lot of church people say, "tight but it's right." When I was a child, I never thought that any of my whippings were right. I remember tightening my butt, hoping it would divert the pain. Of course, that did not work. If you ever had to walk for your own butt cutting ceremony, you would recall some thoughts that were going through your mind. For example, those walks helped you to become acquainted with yourself, and started making you think about when you grow up. It also answered a question like, "Do I like mommy right now?

Sometimes those walks almost made you keep on walking, but you knew that if you tried to run away from home your mom would find you. Especially when it's not that many houses to live in the country. Let's say you go to a neighbor's house. Who do you think the neighbor is going to call after you have eaten their peanut butter and jelly sandwich? Correct! She is going to call your mommy. The peanut butter sandwich was only a cover-up.

As much as those old people like to see you eat back then, more than that, they like to know your business so they can have a say-so in the fussing towards you. Those old people stuck together.

They knew that any child that felt that they were safe and eating a peanut butter sandwich would spill their guts. And depending on what kind of mood they were in, the grown-ups would not give you any snacks. As soon as they saw you calling yourself running away from home, they would start whipping you themselves. They would have no problem taking you to your mom and telling them they just whipped you behind. Of course, back then, your mom would thank her. Right there is where you would wonder if you liked your mom or not for making you walk for your own switch.

You would be red hot angry. You would be angry with the neighbor, of course, and you would be red hot angry with your mom until later that evening when your mom would be in the kitchen cooking. You would be lying in bed with a hot behind and a snotty nose reminiscing on when you had to take that long walk for your own switch, but the smell from the kitchen would fill the entire house. This is how they would get you. A call would come from the kitchen, and it would be your name she was calling. You know you should be still upset, but you know that your mom is the best cook in the whole entire world, and of course, you are not really crazy enough to let her know that you are mad. You answer, yes ma'am. She asks you if you want to lick the spoon or the bowl. This is where you'd lose your mind.

You go running towards the kitchen and you see this serene smile on your mom's face that warms your entire body. That is the image of a mother's love. Then sometimes she would give you a piece of chicken to taste. You think to yourself, wow; I have the best mom in the world, and she isn't too bad, I think I like her. Later that evening when you started eating dinner, you'd forget all about your sore behind and that means an old switch that you had to collect. At that point, the most important thing was that woman that made you walk for that ugly switch knew how to rule a kitchen. As you sat at the table, watching her walk back and forth making sure everyone had enough to eat, a warm feeling would come to you that you could not explain until you came into adulthood, or when your own children come along. That was the facts for me. I can put things into perspective today because of the foundation that was laid for me.

I did not understand it back then, but today I do. My mom was building character in me. She knew that one day she would be gone off the scene. As a child, we want what we want. We don't care if it's good for us or not. Many times, we just don't have a clue. Thank God for wise moms and wise parents.

CHAPTER THREE
Watch Out

One thing I remember as if it was yesterday, was how my mom wanted our undivided attention. When she spoke to you, she wanted you to look right at her. Back in those days, if you turned your back toward your parent while they were talking to you, that was considered disrespectful. Please don't look down on the floor or move your head all around while they are talking to you.

There was a possibility you might not live to tell the story, and if you did, you would remember that moment for the rest of your lives; similar to what I'm doing today. All of those body gestures were not allowed in many of the homes way back then.

"Mop the floor with you."

Now, there was your regular behind cutting and there was a behind cutting that was referred to as, "Mopping the floor with you." This wiping was not your standard butt cutting. No, this was when you tried to find out if any of your friends had a family member that was a lawyer. You know how on those crime solving movies how the people would say, "It's time to lawyer up?" This would be a good time to consider doing just that, lawyer up.

The reason I'm saying that is because by the time your mommy got through with you, you were trying to get yourself up off the floor. During this session of butt whipping, you would be trying to crawl to safety from the floor. At this juncture, your mom wouldn't care what was going on around her and she didn't care who was at the house. Most of the time, this is the type of whipping that left your mom breathing hard and trying to catch her breath, which makes her even more angry.

Around this point is where the mopping up the floor part really manifested, to the peak. In other words, there would be blood in her eyes. So, whenever my mom said, "I'm going to mop the floor with you", I knew it was not going to be pretty.

In Bible college, I learned about twin scriptures. This meant when a scripture from another passage or book in the Bible was either identical to or was saying the same thing as that scripture. Well, I said that to say this. The twin adage to mopping the floor with you was I'm going to trash your behind. Really, those two traveled together because if your mom said that she was going to trash your behind, you got to know that she was going to mop the floor with you. So, in both instances, you would be trying to find a lawyer and getting up from the floor.

However, as a word of advice, I really don't think a lawyer would suffice. Back in the day, those mothers would have beaten the lawyer also and thought nothing of it. The only thing my mom would have said if she would have said anything was, "Sir. You shouldn't have been in the way".

"I'll give you something to cry for."

Picture this, your mom has given you what you consider to be a really descent behind cutting. There you are trying to get yourself together and regain your composure when she walks in the room asking the dumbest question you have ever heard in all your young life of living. "Do you want something to cry for?" Now, you don't dare say it to her face, but deep down in your heart and to the very back of your head you are thinking, is this lady crazy? She just got through mopping the floor with me and trashing my behind, and she wants to know if I want something to cry for. This is all in your head, of course. You continue with your mental monologue.

Unless she is really as crazy as Daddy said, doesn't she know I was just truly crying my eyes out? Without considering all the stuff going through your mind about her conduct, you just look at her and say, "No- no, ma'am!" Now it gets even better. Your mom suggests that to you again, and you think she is a little off her rocker. "Dry it up." There you are trying to do just that, but now that she has made such a major issue of it, you're stressed out. I don't know about you, but this command made me want to fight her. Again, this is yet a monologue in my head. So, what did I do? Looked at her and said, "Yes ma'am." And dried it up!

When I was growing up, the insurance man used to come to your house to collect your few dollars on your life insurance policy. Being that money was so tight back then, I don't know how my mom used to be able to afford to pay, but she did. I believe that was another reason those old people felt such positive energy when it was time to beat our butts. They knew if they killed us, they had it covered. What I'm about to share with you is going to have to stay just between us.

This was a sure thing that could have easily caused me to experience an untimely death, rolling my eyes. As children, the only thing we were thinking was our eyes were just moving because of the stressful situation we were facing or all those crazy questions that they had inflicted upon us. There was no way we could have known that our eyes were contributing to the butt cutting. We really didn't realize it until after a few trial and errors when we were supposed to keep our eyes straight without any movement.

How dare you roll your eyes when your mom was fussing at you? Here comes another crazy question. Do you want those eyes? Here I go back to my monologue in my head. Mommy, you know I'm going to need my eyes in the morning when I put my clothes on for school. What should I say? "Yes ma'am."

For years, I used to ponder a lot of those questions that my mom used to ask me. Sometimes I would wait until I got alone to practice what I would say to her genius questions. The reason I say "genius" questions is because she would look me dead in the eye when she asked those questions. The way I figured it as a child, she must have known her stuff. Her facial expression was on point. I mean, the woman didn't even blink her eyes. Come to think about it, I wonder if she didn't want us to blink our eyes when she was fussing at us. I'm telling you; the woman was a robot.

So, I would fix myself in front of the mirror and practice staring and looking straight. I would hear one of those genius questions of hers in my head. The question would go something like this. "Do you think

I'm crazy?" I would say to myself, I got this one. I watched my mommy for a long time and if anybody knew the answer to that question, it would be me. After all, what would you think the answer would be if the woman that was supposed to be your mom? What is she was the only woman that you ever called mommy made you walk for your own switch to beat your own behind? Would you think that was a lady playing with a full deck? No. That was my answer in my head. Now I know just what to say when she comes to me with that question again. I have thought about it hard and long. Besides, it's a no brainer. The woman was crazy. The case was closed.

When I was about seven years old, I decided to swing on one of our neighbor's screened door. The family was the Reeds. I was having the time of my life. Not one time did the neighbor say anything to me to imply that they did not like me swinging on their screen door. As a matter of fact, they seemed to be happy that I was finding joy out of swinging on their door. Well, I recall something making a noise as I continued swinging. Of course, that didn't stop me because I was having fun. It appeared that one of the hinges loosened and maybe a chain or two became abjured.

Don't ask me how my mom got over to those people's houses so quickly because we did not have a phone in our house. They used to have spies that we knew nothing about because we were children and the only thing on our little minds was having fun. I found out later in life that those spies used to be your own brothers and sisters.

Sometimes the spies would show up as nosey adults that had nothing to do but make little children's life a living hell. The scene was kind of blurry to me as I think about it today, but all I can recollect was my mommy pulling me off the neighbor's screen door and porch asking me one of those questions. "Do you see that screen door?" I didn't have time for one of my mental dialogues in my head, so I answered quickly. Yes, ma'am. Without waiting for an answer from me, she lit into me like a firecracker. All I know is I saw stars. Everybody that was sitting on that porch laughed at me so much you would have thought they were looking at a comedy show.

I was so embarrassed. Back in those days, those parents believed in dealing with you right at the scene of the crime. They wanted you to remember in such a fashion that even after you become an adult, whenever you see that place or thing, you would have a flashback. So, as she held me by one arm, pulling me, my little stick legs were dangling in the air, I started trying to have a logical discussion with her. I knew it was more to the butt cutting when we arrived home, so I thought I could circumvent the matter.

She went on to say things like, "Your daddy doesn't even have a screen door for us, and here you go swinging on somebody's screen door." Now I realized she had just about talked herself into killing me. I had to give it a try. After all, I was her baby and in my little mind, she made me believe that she loved me. So, there I went with my childhood psychology.

She always loved my big, beautiful eyes because that's what that woman told me. I looked up at my mom with those beautiful eyes with the tears rolling down and said to her, "You know mommy, I really didn't mean to swing on Mr. Reed's screen door!" Wait for it! My loving mommy looked right back at me and said, "Do you think I'm crazy?" Remember, I had practiced in the mirror while alone. I had this, and I was prepared. At least that's the way I saw it in my little mind. I saw that woman looking back at me without blinking and her face expression was on point. I knew right there and then; I was going to get the other half of that butt cutting. I answered that crazy woman in the most intelligent fashion I knew. I said to myself, I'm going to really let her have it.

I looked her dead in her eyes and said, "No ma'am- Mommy, you're not crazy!" Well, what else could I say y'all? I might look crazy, but I'm not crazy. Mommy always expected our undivided attention.

Please don't let mommy see you taking your time moving after she has asked you to either go somewhere or to get something for her. My mom used to be a very fast woman. She was easy going and soft-spoken, but that West Indian women could easily move from 1 to 100 easily. She was swift. I remember walking with her to the grocery shop. I hated going to the store with mommy. She would walk so fast. As little and young as I was, I could not keep up with her. She expected you to keep up with her. If she moved, she expected you to be right there in the same spot with her. As I was about to say, Mommy expected you to jump right to it when she asked you to do something. We would be crossing the highway and she would literally drag me across the highway.

When the traffic light would change, she would be like, "Come on, let's run!" Everybody else would be walking taking their time, but my mom would be pulling me because she always thought that Caucasians were looking for an opportunity to hit you with their cars. I thought I was cool back then, so I would move slowly because I was cool. That was not a good idea. Mommy would look at me taking my time and snatch my arm and practically knock me down. She would say, when I say move, you better move. I was so embarrassed.

For some reason, it would always be one of my so-called friends walking by and witnessing mommy snatching me. I knew right there and then I was not going to hear the last of that from my friends because they were going to tease me when we got to the park. However, I realized from that point, to always move when mom wanted me to move. You can always replace your friends, but you cannot replace your arm or your mom. Even though I knew she was crazy, I still wanted to keep her.

CHAPTER FOUR
Just Talking

As the youngest, I was exempted from doing a lot of things around the house. Not only was I the youngest, but like I had mentioned, I was sickly. Therefore, my mom kept a close eye on me and was very careful with my whereabouts and what I do. That was a good thing at times, and it was a not so good thing at other times. For example, I was not allowed to go to my friend's houses for a sleepover like other children because my mom always thought I would get sick, and I would be too far from her.

My mom did baby me a lot, but that did not stop her from taking to my behind as need be. My mom would utilize her daughters for various chores around the house because she had to work. She knew which one of her girls was cut out for whatever task. She had a daughter that she knew would make sure things were straightened up around the house and she knew which one would have the food cooked correctly. This sister really was a superb cook. I wanted to cook something or be as graceful as this sister in the kitchen, but my mom didn't want me to because she feared I would get burned or something would fall on me. I'm not sure, but all I knew was that I was not allowed in the kitchen unless I was accompanied by one of my siblings or Mommy. I remember peeping around the corner and looking toward the kitchen trying to see if the food was ready. My mom would say to me, "A watch pot never cook."

"A Watch Pot Never Cook"

Now, I thought this was a special pot that was used to cook special food. I would have one of those mental monologues with myself. I would say to myself, I don't know why Mommy would use a watch pot in a time such as this when she knows how hungry I was. Doesn't she know that a watch pot takes too long to cook the food because, from what she says, it never cooks? I was beginning to think that Mommy used the watch pot on purpose just to prove to us that we were not the boss of her. Later on in life, I finally learned that my mommy was just being wise at the same time. What she really meant was the more you look and watch the longer it's going to take for the food to cook because of being anxious. That was her way of teaching me patience. The Bible talks about being anxious for nothing. (Philip. 4:6). As children, you want things quickly. Sometimes, as adults, we still want things quickly. My mom always had a quote for every occasion.

My mom made a practice not to comment about so much in front of her children, and when she did, she spoke in what I call in parables. My mom had a keen way of mentioning a person's situation and all their business without calling the person's name. She was just that good, and if by some chance you happened to be somewhere close around and she thought you heard what was said, you bet not repeat it under any circumstances.

Now, that might sound like an easy thing to do or an easy bylaw to follow, but when you are a child, it's not that easy. For one thing, it's not often you get a hold of some grownup information. This information becomes what my mom used to call it, "can't hold water."

"Can't hold water."

You might know some people can't hold water. I happen to know one personally. That person was me as a child. Can't hold water people just couldn't wait to tell whatever they knew. This is where the plot thickens. As my mom would be talking to one of her good friends or her sister, I would have my radar ears cocked towards the conversation. Sometimes, and I mean this did not happen often, but my mom would get caught up in what she is saying and forget about the littles ears that were listening. Like I said, these were rare occasions.

Well, Mommy was in full gear talking to the next-door neighbor one day and some juicy information got out and it fell on my ears. I was one happy camper. I was settled. I had something on the grownups. That's the way my little mind perceived it. After my mom's friend went home, I don't know why I thought this was a good idea, but this was how it went.

This would have been a good time for one of my mental monologues, but for some reason, I think I'm going to blame it on the devil. I decided to let my mom know that I heard what was said because I had the nerve to repeat it word for word.

Not only did I not know how to hold water, but I ended up holding my behind with my hands because my mommy tore my butt up. I learned two valuable lessons that day. One, do not listen in on grownups' conversation. Two, don't repeat what you heard even if you did hear what was said. Oh, yeah, I learned three as a bonus, and that was, whatever you do, please don't repeat it to your mommy.

"That one got all the sense."

Since we are just talking, I remembered Mommy saying, "That one got all the sense." The funny thing about this proverb is it almost sounds like a compliment. As a matter of fact, on a bad day, it could be mistaken for a compliment. I remembered smiling when she would look at me saying those words. I never picked up on her expression looking back at me, which was a strange look. I was only listening to the words. Since I used to get in a lot of mishaps, to hear some nice words made me feel as though I was going to dodge a whipping. To my dismay, the woman was actually calling me a so-called know it all or a little dummy in a kind of nice way. I told you my mommy was a smart woman. Let me set up a scene for you.

I just don't recall what it was I had done, but I know whatever it was, it was worth getting my behind whipped. Mommy had just got through giving me one of those hot behind cuttings, and I was in the corner of the living room. I don't know why it seemed to make you feel like you were someplace else if you could bury yourself in the corner of a wall in your house after a whipping.

It's not like they could not see you or anything, but for whatever reasons, it seemed to be a good idea to get in the corner of any wall in your house after you had a good cry or even while you were crying. It's really crazy now that I am older, but if you were asked or told to go in the corner, you would not like it and you would think it was a crime to be commanded to go to the corner. However, after a good old fashion butt cutting, you automatically found a corner to bury yourself in. One would think of running out of the house or something, but no, most of us just ran to a corner of the house.

However, on one occasion, my mom had just given me one, and there I was backed up in that corner, crying. Well, eventually the sting of the whipping wore off, and I was feeling much better about myself, and I had submerged from the corner. I was back to my old self. You know, when you start to feel better after a butt cutting you start to walk around the house, and you feel your liberty.

Well that did not last too long. My mom's friend came over to visit with her and they started to talk. You know, they were happy to see each other and were laughing and stuff. Now, this would have been a good time for me to excuse myself, but for whatever reason, my little curiosity about hearing what they had to say got the best of me. I stayed right there in the midst trying to act like I was not listening, but really both of my antennas were on high alert to hear the latest gossip. I know, you think I would have learned by now, but no, I was cruising for abusing. This is when I got a full understanding of "that one got all the sense." The conversation made a shift, and for whatever reason, those two old women started talking about their children that just won't listen. My mom's neighbor was getting hot-tempered remembering some things her children had done, and mommy started putting her fifty cents in the pot by telling the women about my business. I found this very upsetting and badly portrayed. My mom always told me not to repeat what I see happening in the house and there she was talking about something that happened in our house. That's when I found out that there were two sets of rules and laws in our house. It was what my mommy said not to say, and it was what my mommy said when she got ready.

However, it went, the children living in the house had no say so. There I was just looking at Mommy telling that lady how bad I was and how she had to let me have it. It went on and on. Just when I thought I had heard enough, as I was about to turn and leave the room, I heard my mommy speaking and pointing at me, "Yeah, and that one right there, she got all the sense!" I went into my mental monologue. I said in my mind," I got you now mommy, you wait to tell your friend to come over to rat me out and make me look like a spectacle. Okay mommy, you just wait.

Call me to do something for you. Just ask me to sweep the floor, pick up my toys, or go to the store to get you a *Mr. Goodbar* or an *Almond Joy*. Just wait mommy, this is war. I kept on walking away from those crazy women. My mommy fixed those warrior eyes on me and yelled at me and told me to stop in my tracks, and of course I did. I'm still having those mental monologues going on in my head. Woman, what do you want now? You done told all my business?

She said, "Play with me and I'll cut your behind again! And get in that room and pick those toys up and get ready to take your bath!" I looked at that old woman and did you know what I said to her? I said, "Yes Ma'am". Yes, that's what I said. Now you might say, that was your time to tell her off. Are you crazy! No one in those neck of the woods was crazier than my soft sweet talking mommy Martha L.S. Green. So, again, I counted my loss and learned another valuable lesson.

I learned that as children, we really do believe we have all the sense. I can understand why mommy said that, and how it became one of her most favorite lines. Rearing children is not easy. Even though I never had a child, I was somebody's child and looking back on my childhood and realizing all the things my mom went through rearing seven children and a granddaughter, could not have been the easiest job in the world. I don't envy her job at all. If anything, I truly commend my mom for not jumping ship. It's an easy thing to walk away, but it takes a whole lot more to stick and stay.

Also, when you have more than one child, you are dealing with more than one personality. Different personalities are a recipe for disaster most of the time. As I have mentioned, my mom was a soft-spoken person with a quiet voice, but if she was pushed to the limit, that voice had a tendency to increase to a tone that you knew was ready for battle. I never liked it when her voice would reach that level. When it did, I knew she was going to give me a one for it or she had enough of my mess. I'm thinking now that I am older, just like the scripture says in the book of Jer. 29:11. God knows the plan that He has for us. God made my mommy in such a fashion because He knew all about the children that were to come into her life. Really, when I was a child, I used to think that I could outsmart my mommy.

I'm sure I was not the only child that thought that way. It seemed that every road I went down, my mom knew about it or knew I was going to take that route. It used to freak me out when I thought of how she was able to stay ahead of me and frustrate me at the same time. I used to think that she had secret eyes that were located behind her head. I'm telling you the truth. That woman could have her back turned to me and still was able to see my move.

I remembered getting ready to reach for something in the house while her back was turned and the woman was in another room, and I would hear her voice echoing from mid-air, "Don't put your hand on it or I'll chop it off!" What? How was she able to do that? Seeing all of that made me not trust her, yet the curious childlike mind of me would push her buttons every time.

I think that was the reason she would always ask us this rhetorical question, "Do you think I'm crazy?". That was her favorite line. As I stated, you really have to watch her face and watch her hands before answering that question. Many times, that was a question that was not meant to be answered. She was really answering the question as she asked it. Now she knew she wasn't crazy, but God had given her some crazy children that didn't know that they were crazy.

I think sometimes my mom used to have a good laugh at all of us at times. After adulthood started approaching, I learned that the reason Mommy knew about those roads that I had taken was because she had walked those very roads before and she had tried many of those tricks that I had thought were so new, on her mom before I even thought about it.

Now the eyes in the back of the head still amazes me to this very day and mommy has been gone on to glory for many, many years now. I guessed that was a combination of knowing her children and once upon a time being a child at one point in her life. My mom had long thick hair and I used to like to play in her hair, but most of all, I was trying to locate those extra eyes. I never found them.

My mom had never had her hair cornrows before, but when it was almost her departure from this side, she allowed me to cornrow her hair for her one day. I thought that was the coolest thing. I had one of my mental monologues. I said, "Finally, I will find those secret hidden eyes now mommy. Who is the smartest and the crazy one now, Mommy?" I will always remember that. Again, as I was braiding her hair, I was convinced that would be the day that I would put all the knowing my moves in advance at rest. I would part her hair and look, part some more hair, and look. I was looking for those extra eyes, but I never found them. So, I concluded, the woman was just that smart. Yes, Mommy, what were you really saying?

As a child, you'd always think that you had one up on your parents. It never entered our little heads that our parents were once children also, and it never occurred to us that games we tried to play were not new games, but just new players.

We were, as children, the new players with the same old games. As I look back over my life, I can truly appreciate all the times when I thought my mom was crazy and I can also appreciate her not allowing me to run wild, as many of my friends in the neighborhood. I really wanted to go to some of those cool places and do some of what I thought were cool things, but I most certainly can appreciate that crazy woman that was my mom that did not allow me to be cool. I say crazy, but she was crazy like a fox.

"Dry It Up Before I Knock You Into Next Week"

Have you ever cried so long and so much until you get that double sniffle sound from your nose as you try to catch your breath after a real good behind cutting? Most of you know exactly what I'm talking about. Well, I could have easily printed the letters for the t-shirt for that one. Now, I already gotten what I thought was the butt cut of the century and my mom walks into the room and looks at me with those hell and brimstone eyes and says to me, "Dry it up before I give you something to cry about." Excuse me! Now I'm really confused.

Can't this woman see I'm going through a crisis? Here I am trying to get myself together because she just knocked the wind out of me and I can hardly gather my composure, and she is threatening me with more bodily harm. Really? This is the time to have another one of my personal mental monologues. I say to myself, "Lady, if you put your hands on me one more time, it's going down in here. And it will be hell to pay if you think I'm going to let you even come close to me again! You got another thing coming." But what did I say to her when I responded? "Yes, yes. Ma'am." Like I said, I used to have a lot of those mental conversations in my head. I think that is what helped me to start writing.

Telling a child to dry it up while you got a good cry going was about the worst until you are told that if you don't hush and stop crying, you are going to get knocked into next week.

The first time my mom said that to me, I really thought she was talking to someone else. Don't ask me who I thought that other person was. All I know is there was no way she was talking to me. Remember, I was thinking with a tiny child's brain, but even at that juncture, I knew there was something wrong with that comment. I remember her asking me if I heard what she said.

Again, occasionally I would dismiss things that she said to me so I would be able to try to process it before opening my mouth. I was so appalled by such a gesture until I was lost for words. I really wanted to ask her, "Mommy, how do you figure to do that?" Now, I knew better to say that out loud or to even think I could be at liberty to ask such a question and live.

I immediately went into one of my mental monologues. Is this why some of the children in the neighborhood are missing? Is it possible that the parents knocked them into next week and that is the reason for them being missing from the playground?

Mommy had no idea the stress she put on me by that statement. She must have felt the shift in the atmosphere because, for some reason, she just looked at me for a long time and allowed me to quietly go to my room. Normally, she would wait for me to give her an answer like, "Yes ma'am" but I think I freaked her out that day with a hazed look on my face. I just could not imagine being knocked so hard that I would end up in another time span.

Most of the things Mommy said to me I could sometimes fit together. However, that one caught me off guard. Of course, as I got older, I found out that my mom knew I was freaked out by her comment that she had to excuse herself to her room, where she laughed her head off. What a cruel thing to do to your child? Mommy, what were you really saying?

While it is true that for most reasons, children will say one thing with the mouth and have a whole different scene going on in their head. I should know because I was guilty of that on many occasions. Back in those days, it was not the thing for children to be a part of the grown-up conversations or to think they were welcome to sit in the midst of the parents' company. I said that to say this.

If your mom or dad had a friend to come over to visit with them for whatever reasons, as a child, even if you were in the living room at the time of the company's visitation, that was your cue to excuse yourself. It was not so much as where to go when your parent's friends showed up as much as it was an issue of you making sure you do not find yourself in the same space as your parent's friends. It was an automatic built in policy that was unwritten. Now you are probably wondering how we were able to pick up on that without rehearsal. This is the thing; it was extended from trial and error.

A long time before my mom would have company over, she had already drilled into us that we were not to be in her company, and to sit up in grown folks' company showed a sign of disrespect and wanting to be grown before time. Moreover, she would stress that if caught in her business, she would let us have it. Now, those are piercing words that stay with you. No child wants to endure that kind of anguish.

So, most of the time, we try to abide by her wishes. Without explanations, it's just something about grown-up conversations that seems to pull on you. I mean after all, we were children, and it's not like we had so much going on in our lives, so the big people's lives were very instructive to us. I know that was the case for me. Therefore, for some crazy reasons, I would forget that I should've been excusing myself from the grown-up's conversation. However, it was just those times when my little ears would catch something, and it would fashion some invisible glue to my butt, and I would not be able to move from my seat. So, what did I do? I pretended that I had forgotten the in-service that mommy went over with me and just decided to act like I was busy doing something and not really listening to them, but all the while, my little ears were cocked to the conversation.

I would overhear things like, "Sis, you know dat gal leg broke again, and she didn't forget' no husband" Now, while this sounds really good, I don't really get it. Remember, I was a child and many times my mom and her friends would speak a dialect that was beyond my comprehension. Some of it extended from our Gullah roots.

Later, I found out they purposely spoke that way because they knew that little ears were listening, and all close eyes were not asleep. That's what Mommy used to say. When I heard the girl's leg was broken. I started to feel bad for her. Even though I didn't know the person, I knew that it had to be a bad thing to have a broken leg.

Now that was my interpretation of what I heard. It was not until I got a little older that I found out that the young girl's leg was not actually broken at all. My mom was saying that it was a young unwed girl that had gotten pregnant for the second time. Who would have known? My mom used to say the darndest things.

CHAPTER FIVE

"When I was a child, I spoke as a child, I understood as a child, I thought as a Child: but when I became a man, I put away childish things." (1 Cor. 13:11).

When I was a child, I remembered people, situations, and toys that seemed to be bigger than they actually were. I remembered a special spot located in our kitchen that was next to our old wood stove. It seemed to me at the time as a large space, but in reality, it was a small space that welcomed a small person. I used to play in that space with my toys as I kept an eye on mommy.

For whatever reason, I thought it was my job to try to keep up with my mom's every move. In my little head, I wanted to stay close just in case she decided to go somewhere, I was sure to follow. I was just like Mary's Little Lamb. You see, I was a child, I thought as a child. I could not think beyond that scope because my thinking process was limited.

The writer Apostle Paul was making a comparison of immaturity and maturity in (1 Cor.

13:11). One of the points was that when your mentality is that of a child, you see things on that level, but as you grow and mature, you begin to see things differently because your understanding is reaching from a more developed area. I said all of that to say this, when you are a child, you hear things and see things on a child level. Things seem to take on a more colorful atmosphere.

Things seem to preoccupy the space in your head as opposed to when you are older. There are things that rocked your world when you were a child. However, when you look back in hindsight, all you can do is laugh at yourself, and sometimes be slightly embarrassed. That was the transitional period in your growing life.

As I was growing up listening to my mom say the things that she said it felt like I was opening a pirate's treasure. It was unlocking a new world to me. I didn't understand that some of the times she knew I could have been listening. She aimed to confuse me by speaking in parables. Our house was a very small house and there wasn't much space to make yourself scarce, especially if it was raining outside. Most of the time, Mommy would expect you to go outside somewhere under the tree or something when the weather was good and when one of her friends came by. On the other hand, if the weather was not good, I excused myself to one of the small rooms in our little house. In our house the walls had holes in them and the only insulation was between your ears and your eyes, if you get what I'm saying.

When I was a child, it was second nature for me to look where I shouldn't look and listen when I shouldn't listen. All of that goes back to immaturity and just being a child. There wasn't a manuscript that came along with you at birth no more than a manual that came along with your parents. Like I said, it was like a pirate's treasure. It made me feel good to think that I was possessing something from the adult script. It made me feel empowered to know something that none of the other children knew.

However, it didn't feel so good when I had to pay the piper. It was so amazing to me when I was a child to think that it was just a matter of time when those grown-ups would find out that you were eavesdropping, or as what they called it, "being nosey." That was another adage that my mom used to throw around. "Being nosey." This is when you had a piece of juicy information that usually ended up with a sore behind. Sometimes the information that you came upon was worth the behind cutting. I used to look at it like this. You might cut my behind, but now I still know who is really pregnant. You had to be a robust child in those days because those old people would interrogate you, and if you were not strong, you would end up losing your best friend.

The reason I said that you would end up losing your best friend is the fact that by the time my mom got through with telling me about her hard times that she went through as a child, and how her mom died from a broken heart, I would end up giving up my best friend in exchange for the interrogation to stop. You would be standing there with tears rolling down your eyes saying things like, "No ma'am, I was not alone when I did it." And there goes your best friend up the creek without a paddle. Now your best friend is going to get a whipping from her parents for lying. Anybody who is anybody knows that is the one thing you did not want to be caught in was a lie. It is best to get a head start. Start taking off your good clothes because they paid good money for those clothes, and they are not going to take a chance ripping them up or that will be an extra lick.

Seemed like those chastisements went on for hours, but really it wasn't too long because most of the time my mom would be tired out. She would start sweating and then she would get angry about sweating as if it was my fault. Parents can be very peculiar. Now, after the sweat, she would usually find the nearest chair to sit down. This is where phase two comes into play. Phase two is when she is too tired to continue spanking you, but she keeps talking about it and going over the reason she spanked you while she keeps her eyes on you. Those eyes seemed like it was penetrating through my clothes and my body. Sometimes it would be in your best interest to move slowly out of her presence. Now, you might say, why leave? She is tired and only talking. That's a trap. Even though she is tired for the moment, she is rehearsing the moment and reminiscent, out of nowhere, she will regain strength. The more she talks about the reason she had to tear your behind up, she's going to get angry all over again. If you are still in her reach, she is going to grab your behind again and you will think the incredible Hulk had a hold of you. That is why it's in your best interest to get out of that lady's sight.

I remember Mommy in a special way. When I was a very little girl, I used to watch my mom sew. She did not own a sewing machine or anything, but she would sew with her hands. I remember her mending stuff. For example, if a sock or a dress needs altering or just patched up because money was tight and very slow to come by, Mommy would take care of it herself.

She wasn't able to take it to any seamstress or anything. Mommy really did a good job keeping our clothes mended. My most memorable moment of Mommy sewing was this can that she used to take out doing her time of sewing. It was called a "button can." It was a brown can with a brown top. The top fitted really tight on the can, so you had to put your muscle into it when removing it. What I loved about that can was the things inside the can.

There were all kinds of beautiful buttons in that can. What was amazing about those buttons was the fact that a story went with each button. It was astonishing to me how Mommy was able to remember the stories. Seems like she didn't mind me asking her about the buttons. It all started one day when Mommy was looking for a button to replace on a shirt.

Mommy took out that old brown can and emptied the buttons on the bed and as she pushed through the buttons one by one, she began what became a ritual for us. Mommy selected a button that matched the buttons on the shirt, which I found quite magical. I said "Mommy, that button looks just like the button on the shirt." Mommy looked at me and smiled. Mommy said, "Do you know that this button came off one of your daddy's working shirts when he used to work on the railroad?" My eyes would stretch, and I would exclaim, "No, Mommy. Did daddy work on the train tracks?" By this time, her smile turned into a laugh. She said, "No baby." I realized as I got older, it wasn't what

I said as much as how I said it. Back in those days, black men were responsible for the trains, the cargos, and many other things that went along with working for the railroad.

Mommy went on with her story of how my daddy's shirt became so old until she had to start using it for a cleaning rag. But before turning it into a cleaning rag, she popped all the buttons of the shirt and placed them in the button can. In those days, you just didn't throw away something, you utilized it for something else. Today we call it recycling. Then I would point to certain buttons and the lesson began. Mommy, what about this button? It would be a pretty button that almost looks like a button that could have been on Cinderella's dress.

Mommy would have this faraway look on her face, and she would start smiling again. She said, "This button came off this fancy dress that I had when your daddy and I were real young." I'm always interrupting her by asking her, "Mommy, was I born yet?" As many times I've asked her this very same question, she seems to never get angry. She would slow the story down and say, "No baby, you were not born yet." She would pick up where she left off. "I used to dress up in that dress and put on my high heels and get ready to go to the revival. That was such a beautiful dress. I loved that dress." Mommy would say.

Now in my little mind, I would be thinking, you wore that beautiful dress to church. But back in Mommy's day, going to revivals was fun for her. Mommy was passionate about her Jesus. That's how I came to love the Lord. I would go on and on with the many questions as I saw buttons that were either pretty to me or just peculiar. Mommy had a story for each button I chose. Of course, this was before I was born. Mommy told me about her wedding dress. Oh, how I wish I could see that dress.

Mommy told me how long the train was and how it took about three or four people to help hold it up as she walked down the aisle. She said her veil went all the way down her back. I said, "Mommy, where is your wedding dress?" She said, "I cut it up and made beautiful dresses for your sisters. I got silent. I thought to myself, wow, they must have looked really pretty in Mommy's wedding dress. I wondered if they knew that mommy sacrificed her wedding dress for them. Mommy, what were you really saying?

"I Clean Forgot"

Mommy said a lot of things when I was a child. I remember mommy saying things like "I clean forgot." Now clean forgetting something is not like just forgetting about a thing. It was almost like one was begging the other because even though they forgot to do whatever, their heart was pure. In other words, their intentions were all about you, but at the same time. Something honestly kicked any memory of whatever you needed them to do right out of their mind. They didn't have any animosity in their heart when they forgot to do whatever for you because they just forgot.

The forgetting was like the reverse of an act of kindness, but just in the opposite way. If you would put it in a conversation, it would sound like this. "I know I had to pick you up, but I clean forgot." Yes, I know you needed to get to the store before it closed, but I clean forgot." Yeah, you are right, I should have put aside some tuna salad before it all ran out, but I clean forgot." It's almost like you can hear the cry for help in the explanation. See, when a person includes the term, "clean forgot," it is supposed to make you understand that they had a very good reason for letting you get wet up in the rain even though you reminded them to make sure to put your umbrella in the car before leaving the house.

Therefore, this "clean forgetting" should be understood that the person didn't wish any harm to come to you. The fact of the matter is that what is at hand is not found anywhere in their memory banks. Again, if it was just merely forgetting something, that would be another story with a unique twist.

When you have one of those people in your family that often "clean forgets" please do yourself a favor and try never to ask them to do anything for you because you will most certainly end up with the short end of the stick. The short end of the stick brings me to another thing I used to hear my mommy say.

"The Short End of The Stick."

What does it mean to end up with the short end of the stick? Do I want a short stick and what would I use a short stick for? Would there come a day when a short stick would be fashionable? As a child, when you hear certain things being said, you often roll it around in your head to try and make sense of it. Now, when I first heard my mom say, "Child, you don't wanna end up with the short end of the stick" I immediately envisioned a long stick turning into a short stick for no reason except it possibly should not have been long in the first place.

I had no idea my mom was referring to a situation. Now I remember my mom telling me that if you choose a stick to fight with, the stick should not be longer than your forearm, and with that being said, I was a bit mixed up. Of course, I managed to separate the two as I continued to stick around my mom. Mommy was saying to be wise and watch yourself. On another note, Mommy was saying, not to be nobody's fool. In those days, I guess it would have taken too much time to say things the way we articulate today. So, Mommy just said it the way she heard it or the way she understood it and that was okay with me.

CHAPTER SIX

Are you hungry?

"Stomach going to my back."

This sounds like someone in need of some serious medical attention. Well, when something like this is said, this person is trying to let you know that they are really hungry. If my mommy said, get out of her way because her stomach is gone to her back, everyone knew to move out of Mommy's way because she was hungry and in need of some food right away. If you get in her way by trying to ask a question about anything, you would be getting in between a crossfire and would be putting yourself in danger of getting knocked into next week.

Back to your stomach going to your back. This was when you were so hungry, if someone offered you some nails, you might try to eat them. When your stomach is going to your back, no one can stop you from getting something in your stomach because that's all that matters at that appointed time.

"A hungry man ain't choosy."

I remember when I was little, I used to go up to my mommy and say, "Mommy, I'm hungry." My mom would say, "Go fix yourself a peanut butter and jelly sandwich. I would say, "I don't want a peanut butter and jelly sandwich." My mom would look at me and say, "A hungry man ain't choosey." All I could think of at the time was my mommy sees I'm hungry, and she chose a time like now to tell me a story about a choosy man. I did not understand that my mom was making a significant statement.

Again, I'm rolling this thing around in my little mind. I'm crying and thinking my mom is the worst mom in the world and she is not concerned about feeding her hungry little girl, and she calls herself a mom. What is wrong with this lady? I thought she loved me and here she is allowing me to go hungry and roll around on this floor and I'm dying of hunger.

This was a mighty lesson for me to learn, and I am so grateful. My mom walked past my limp and crying body and went on with whatever she was doing, as if she couldn't see me. So, when I finally calmed down and understood in my little mind that I wasn't going to get anything else to eat except the peanut butter and jelly sandwich, I got up off the floor. I wiped my face, blew my nose, and fixed that sandwich. I was a happy camper. Mommy meant that if I was as hungry as I said, I would not have a problem with eating whatever was offered to me. The moral of the hungry man not being choosy. I was introduced to the hungry, choosy man that day.

"Thought Like Nellie."

Often, while talking with her friends, I would hear my mom say, "Thought like Nellie." Then they would lean back with a belly of laughter. Now, when I would hear juicy things like this, it would make me hungry to find out exactly what they meant by "thought like Nellie." Who was Nellie and where was she from, and was Nellie a great thinker? It never ceases to amaze me how something so simple can have such a relevant meaning when my mom expresses it. While I never learned where Nellie was from or if she was a great thinker, I later learned what Nellie was and that if you think like Nellie, you were either not too bright or you didn't take the time to think something through before opening your mouth.

Normally, when the old people called Nellie to the stage, they were demonstrating how you need to take a good look at Nellie and not make the same mistake that Nellie made by talking out of terms or not being more aware of her surroundings. Nellie was one of those adages that was used to let those that were within hearing distance know that someone was taken advantage of in the worst way.

How I'm able to come to such a conclusion concerning the Nellie thing is the fact that there was a second part to the "Thought like Nellie "adage. The second part was almost like an answer to a question, and it could have easily gone like this. "Yeah girl, they thought like Nellie, and you know what Nellie was right? Yeah, Nellie was a fool."

That's how I was introduced to Nellie. I found out when my mom and her friends wanted to make a point concerning the absence of brain matter within a person without just coming out calling them out of their name or referring to them as not making a wise decision.

They would actually mention the person indirectly, but never just come right out and call the person a fool, but rather recite this backyard poem. They would explain what the person had done, but at the end of the story, they would say, "Thought like Nellie, and you know what Nellie was right? Yeah, Nellie was a fool."

While it was my mom and her friends' way of making a point, I later found out it was the highlight of a story just so they could have a big laugh. Mommy, what were you really saying?

"Don't chew your fat twice."

This was one of those sayings that made me laugh out loud just to hear it. Again, as usual, I would be eavesdropping in on big people's conversations. I heard my mom say that she doesn't believe in chewing her fat twice. Now when you are a child and certain things are said in such a fashion until it lingers in your mind. That's when your little mind starts to wonder. I was one of those children that had a big imagination. So, I started to visualize my mom chewing on some fat meat.

From my perspective, it really didn't make much sense for my mom to waste time chewing on fat and not the meat. Not to mention, she was double chewing for no reason at all. The more I thought about it, the less it made any sense to me. Even though my mom could do and say some crazy things, I didn't really think she was crazy.

Now, that was a question that she asked me all the time, so I finally realized that if a mom asked you that question all the time, she probably had good sense. She just wanted to get in your little heads. Back to chewing your fat twice. I later learned that my mom was not talking about food at all. It's not like I could have gone up to mommy and asked her what she meant, because then I would have had to explain to her where I got that information from.

Of course, that would have been one of those tricky questions. Regardless of how I answered it, she would have known I was eavesdropping on her conversation, and that would be a recipe for some strong reprimand.

My mom was actually saying that she was not a woman to repeat herself. Dah. Was that too hard to say to mommy? I don't know why she just couldn't come right out and say that.

It seemed like such a long way around, but that was the way my mom talked. As I got older, and remembered how my mom always used to say, "Don't make me say it again" or "Don't make me talk". It all makes sense to me as an adult. Mommy was saying all along that she wouldn't chew her fat twice. In other words, please make sure you listen closely the first time.

CHAPTER SEVEN
Knowing When To Shut Up

"Don't Make Me Talk"

That was another adage that Mommy occasionally used to get her point across. What my mommy was saying was she had a hard day working in those white folks' homes and she was talked out. Moreover, she had to clean their home and run behind those little white children while trying to keep them in line. Many times, she had to spank their little butts. Therefore, she was not in any mood for foolishness from any of her brown babies.

For some reason, Mommy was looking in my direction. So, I knew right then that whatever my questions were, I better make it plain and short. Mommy had done a lot of talking all day on her job and she was making her declaration that as much as we might know her to have plenty of words, her cut off point was very close. We needed to understand that she was subject to explode. This was not a threat. It wasn't like she would ban us to the island of Patmos, but it would be a pity to pay if the line was crossed.

Just one more question, one more comment, or one more complaint might have sent Mommy to the moon. Mommy needed some quiet time. She needed some self-time. Mommy needed to sit back and just relax for a moment, even if it was just to be able to collect her thoughts. Even though that was a nice request, Mommy rarely got it. While having a lot of children, the last thing you might experience is total quietness when getting home from work.

If we started any type of argument amongst one another, that was when we heard those four favorite words:" Don't make me talk." It was amazing because when we would hear Mommy say those words, right away we knew to bring everything to a fast halt. I think it was the character David Banner from the series, *The Incredible Hulk* who would say, "Don't make me angry because you would not like me if I got angry." Of course, they would not listen to him because standing before them was this clean-cut small frame of a man that looked like he wouldn't hurt a fly. Well, he got mad because they kept on pushing him, and this is where the real story kicks in. If I remember correctly, his head would turn toward the people that had gotten on his nerves and his eyes changed color. He would start to burst out of his shirt as the buttons did their own thing. By that time, you would see this small frame of a man start to morph into this Hercules like being.

David Banner's face would change to a green color, and I think his eyes turned red. This was David Banner who had changed into the Incredible Hulk right in front of the same people that he told to leave him alone and to not make him angry. Now he is picking up cars and pulling trees up from the root. He is throwing things around, and the people that he warned to leave him alone are now running for cover. They're thinking he is a mad man with no sense.

Actually, they were correct. He was mad because he told them not to make him angry. The same thing with my mom. If we kept on pushing her and pushing her she would end up turning into the Incredible Mommy Hulk. She warned us. She said, "Don't make me talk." I hope I was able to paint a clear canvas of my mommy when she used those four words, "Don't make me talk."

After we saw her popping out of her clothes a few times and reach for her belt, we got the picture. We eventually understood that when Mommy got home from work, she needed to chill for a while before we decided to bomb rush her.

Don't get me wrong, Mommy was a sweet and loving woman, and she loved her children. Back in those days, things were hard, and money was so tight, and even worse for black people. My father was there, but he was not a punctual father. That caused my mommy to wear an extra pair of shoes to make sure her children were taken care of. My father, on the other hand, is another book all by itself, but back to my point.

Mommy, you taught me so much as a child and it seemed that you spoke in parables. In fact, you did-because it was much needed during that time. That is why I asked you, Mommy, what were you really saying?

THE END